Dog Nu  for Beginners

Beginner's Guide to Dog Nutrition and Homemade Meal Recipes so You Can Feed Your Pet With Good and Healthy Stuff While Avoiding the Bad and Unhealthy Stuff

By Norman Thornton

© **Copyright 2021 - All rights reserved.**

The content contained within this book may not be reproduced, duplicated or transmitted without direct written permission from the author or the publisher.

Under no circumstances will any blame or legal responsibility be held against the publisher or author for any damages, reparation, or monetary loss due to the information contained within this book. Either directly or indirectly.

Legal Notice:

This book is copyright protected. This book is only for personal use. You cannot amend, distribute, sell, use, quote or paraphrase any part, or the content within this book, without the consent of the author or publisher.

Disclaimer Notice:

Please note the information contained within this document is for educational and entertainment purposes only. All effort has been executed to present accurate, up to date and reliable, complete information. No warranties of any kind are declared or implied. Readers acknowledge that the author is not engaging in the rendering of legal, financial, medical or professional advice. The content within this book has been derived from various sources. Please consult a licensed professional before attempting any techniques outlined in this book.

By reading this document, the reader agrees that under no circumstances is the author responsible for any losses, direct or indirect, which are incurred as a result of the use of information contained within this document, including, but not limited to, —errors, omissions, or inaccuracies.

Contents

Introduction 1
   The Key Advantages of a Good Eating Plan 1
   Homemade Dog Food 2
Chapter 1: Feeding Your Dog 4
   Eating Plan 4
   Necessary Nutrients 6
      Carbohydrates 6
      Proteins 7
      Minerals 7
      Vitamins 8
      Fat 9
      Fiber 9
   Balancing Act 10
   How Much Food Does My Dog Need? 10
   Keeping an Eye on the Calories 11
   When to Feed My Dog? 12
   Feeding Advice 13
   Types of Food 14
Chapter 2: Is Homemade Dog Food Any Good? 22
   Well balanced Diet 23
   Supplementation 26
   Time and Expense 27
   Storage and Shelf-life 28
   Homemade Recipes 29

- Homemade Dog Food Kinds 31
  - Raw Dog Food VS Biologically Appropriate Raw Food (BARF) 31
  - Organic Homemade Dog Food 32
  - Homemade Holistic Dog Food 33
- Should You Give Supplements to Your Dog? 34
- Should You Be Cooking For Your Dog? 36

Chapter 3: Homemade VS Store-Bought Dog Food 38
- Nutrition 38
- Selection 39
- Management 40
- Cost 41
- Which Is More Affordable? 42
  - Canned Dog Food 42
  - Dry Dog Food 43
  - Homemade Dog Food With Ordinary Ingredients 43
  - Homemade Dog Food With Organic Ingredients 44
- Myths and Misconceptions 44
- Warning 50

Chapter 4: Recipes 52
- Veggie and Beef Balls 53
- Vegetable and Turkey Supper 54
- Chicken Casserole 56
- Dog Chili 58
- Peanut Butter Cookies 59
- Chicken Jerky 62

Frozen Yogurt Pops 63

Vegetable and Fruit Strips 64

Chapter 5: Foods to Give/Avoid 67

    People Foods That are Safe for Dogs 68

        Lean Meat 68

        Raw (and cooked) Eggs 68

        Fruits 69

        Veggies 69

        Baked potatoes 70

        Pasta and White Rice 70

    Risky Human Food 72

        Alcohol 72

        Apple Seeds 72

        Avocado 73

        Baby food 73

        Bones 73

        Sweet and Gum 74

        Cat food 74

        Chocolate 74

        Citrus Extracts 75

        Coffee 75

        Corn on the Cob 75

        Fat Trimmings 76

        Fish 76

        Grapes and Raisins 77

        Human Vitamins 77

- Liver 77
- Macadamia Nuts 78
- Milk and Dairy 78
- Mushrooms 78
- Onions, Garlic, and Chives 79
- Persimmons, Peaches, and Plums 79
- Rhubarb and Tomato leaves 80
- Raw fish 80
- Salt 80
- Sugar 81
- Tobacco 81
- Xylitol 82
- Yeast (by itself or in dough) 82
- Old Food 83
- Leftovers 83
- Take a look at the Ingredients 83
- Human Snacks 84

When In Doubt, Talk to a Veterinarian 84

Thank you for buying this book and I hope that you will find it useful. If you will want to share your thoughts on this book, you can do so by leaving a review on the Amazon page, it helps me out a lot.

Introduction

Selecting the best sort of dog food you offer is most likely the most crucial choice you are going to ever make for your dog- senior or pup. Dog food nutrition immediately affects every element of your dog's life. Elements like how puppies grow, their habits, health, total wellness and physical look are all firmly connected to the nutrition dog owners supply. It goes without saying, this is a huge obligation.

The Key Advantages of a Good Eating Plan

A well-balanced, healthy dog food eating plan promotes:

- Healthy coat and skin

- Clear, bright eyes

- Strong bones and muscles

- Great oral health

- More firm stool

- Burst of energy

- Less indigestion

- Excellent way of life

- Barely any behavior issues

- Long life

Homemade Dog Food

Given the most recent news regarding dog food recall and associated problems with commercial dog foods, the homemade dog food option has actually come to the leading edge.

Preparation of your dog's meals from the ground up has many advantages, and that includes complete control of all meals served. You understand exactly what enters into every meal and where the produce and components were sourced, in addition to understanding that it has actually been prepared in good environments.

It does require an arranged individual to create a homemade feeding strategy, and after that, make all of the daily dog meals. Typical homemade dog meals consist of healthy soups, huge meaty stews, veggies and possibly some raw bones every now and then. The homemade dog food option likewise has actually the included responsibility of creating nutritionally well-balanced meals, and dealing with the calorie needs for your dog. If you equip yourself with the appropriate recipes, veterinarian's approval and get involved in a program, this practice isn't all that tough to maintain.

Chapter 1: Feeding Your Dog

To maintain your dog's health condition, it's crucial to feed him using a healthy eating plan and the appropriate quantity of it daily. There is a wide array of canine foods offered, so it could be difficult to choose. There are, nevertheless, specific dietary nutrients which a dog can't do without - protein, fat, carbs, vitamins, fiber, minerals, and water, along with age, health and way of life elements to think about, and this assists in making the job of selecting the most appropriate eating plan less hard.

Eating Plan

Dogs are omnivorous in the feeding routines and could do with specifically developed vegetarian eating plan programs, even though they do like meat-based meals a lot more. In a wild state, the dog hunts, kills, feeds, and then rests. He might pack himself on an entire animal one day, and after that, go without food for the following 2 or 3 days; this is why a great deal of dogs are eager to consume food up until they're fit to burst - instinct lets them know they might need to hold out for a long time prior to their next mealtime.

Adult domestic dogs are typically fed once daily, however, splitting that feed into 2 meals includes interest and relationship. It's likewise more effective to feed particular deep-chested types, such as Great Danes, German Shepherds, and Setters, a number of little meals instead of one huge one, to prevent possibly terminal gastrointestinal conditions like bloating.

You are going to discover retail-produced medical eating plans offered, normally just accessible from vets, which can help dogs dealing with a wide variety of illnesses, such as indications of senility, kidney stones, gastrointestinal disruptions, weight problems, diabetes, mellitus, and gum and tooth issues. There are even food products made for long-coated types, along with life-stage solutions. You might likewise select from holistic eating plans in which have no artificial ingredients and eating plans developed for allergic reaction victims.

Necessary Nutrients

Normally, dogs aren't hard to feed, and they prosper on an eating plan not truly distinct to people, albeit with a bit more protein. Most of the foods of animal origin, root veggies, cereal items and fats are simple for them to digest. The trick of appropriate feeding is to provide a well-balanced eating plan that offers all necessary goodness in the proper percentages to each other with the objective designated - work, development, breeding or healthy adulthood. These kinds of nutrients are listed beneath:

Carbohydrates

Carbohydrates offer approximately 70% by weight of the dog's food (after removing any water) or around two-thirds of the calories. Dog biscuits, rice and pasta are 3 beneficial energy foods for dogs, and rice is a beneficial food product for dogs that are allergic to wheat.

Proteins

Proteins inside plants and meat (even though the latter is substandard to the former) enhance body tissue, perform "repair work," and create hormones. The dry matter of dog food should consist of a minimum of 15% protein, of which the bulk ought to originate from animal foods (dairy and meat items), or top quality veggie protein such as soya.

Minerals

Minerals are periodically described as "ash" on dog-food labels. The important ones are phosphorus, calcium and sodium chloride (common salt) in a healthy mix. Phosphorus and calcium make up the majority of the mineral matter of bone and need to be used at the rate of about 3% calcium/phosphorus in the eating plan; an extreme quantity of calcium in the eating plan, especially in large-breed pups, can lead to skeletal abnormalities, while an extreme quantity of phosphorus (discovered in offal eating plans and high meat) might possibly trigger eclampsia in lactating female dogs.

Crucial minerals for good health, such as copper and zinc, arise naturally in cereals and meat, in addition to other elements of a well-balanced eating plan.

Vitamins

Vitamin A (likewise referred to as retinol) is necessary for vision and development, while vitamins of the B group are essential for the maintenance, particularly, of the nerve system.

Vitamin D helps the body to produce calcium, needed for healthy teeth and bones, as is phosphorus. Vitamin E (tocopherol) is essential for the leveling of cell membranes. Considering that dogs can develop their own vitamin C (ascorbic acid, important for preserving healthy skin and connective tissue), this does not always need to come with an eating plan.

Fat

Fat adds to food palatability, however, it remains, in reality, just as vital as a source of the important fats (EFAs, likewise called polyunsaturates), which are important to overall health. They generally work by managing water loss via the skin. A shortage in EFAs can result in reproductive, coat, skin and injury healing issues.

Fiber

A lack of fiber in the eating plan might result - especially in non-active, elderly dogs - in bowel issues and other gastrointestinal issues triggered by slow bowels. Fiber is offered via the indigestible plant matter in foods such as raw and cooked veggies in addition to cereals.

Balancing Act

It's vital that the balance of nutrients offered to a dog is proper, considering that excesses might trigger as many health concerns as insufficiencies. If your dog gets more calories every day than his body needs, he is going to get fat. Just as in people, obesity is behind lots of canine diseases, such as heart issues, decrease in lung function and joint disorders.

How Much Food Does My Dog Need?

This depends on your animal's:

- Activity level
- Size
- Character
- Age
- Temperature of environments

Young pups and those being worked, or which are truly active daily, might need more food daily than the typical pooch, while an non-active, old dog is going to require less.

Keeping an Eye on the Calories

Energy is determined in heat units referred to as calories. In a healthy dog, the quantity of calories he needs levels out the amount of calories that his body utilizes daily. In case this balance is well maintained, the dog remains fit and healthy and his weight stays stable. An underfed dog progressively drops weight as his body pulls on the reserves of protein and fat to comprise the deficiencies in his eating plan.

The quantity of calories a dog requires day-to-day depends on its size, activity level, life phase, and uniqueness. As an instance, a small healthy adult dog with 2 hours of routine activity a day needs anything in between 130 and 700 calories every day depending upon its size; a huge dog is going to require from 1,500 daily.

Pups need more calories since they're growing promptly, have a tendency to be more prone to heat loss due to their little size, and their energy needs are higher. Nursing female dogs need some 50 to 60% more calories than typical, and extremely active (working) dogs need a minimum of 40% more calories than typical reasonably energy needs.

When to Feed My Dog?

The majority of owners feed either during the night or morning and frequently both, identified by their dog's specific preferences or age requirements. Some dogs fare much better with their day-to-day provision broken into 2 or perhaps 3 meals, while some are delighted to consume their everyday allowance in simply a single helping, offering it's not a danger for them to do so.

It's ideal not to feed adult dogs at identical times every day, because depending on a stiff regimen can disturb the dog if you get home late and aren't able to offer him food at the anticipated time.

Feeding Advice

Here are a couple of fundamental rules to stick to when feeding your dog:

- Put paper or a feeding mat, beneath feeding bowls, given that lots of dogs are careless eaters.

- It is suggested to present modifications to the eating plan bit by bit to protect against intestinal tract issues.

- Never ever provide spiced food or that to which any alcohol has actually been included.

- To stay clear of choking, eliminate all bones from fresh fish and meat.

- Fresh, tidy drinking water needs to constantly be accessible.

- Ensure water and food bowls are constantly tidy.

- Never enable your dog to take in chocolate meant for human usage, as it's harmful to them.

- Consult your veterinarian if your dog shows any unwillingness to drink or eat.

- Deter your dog from begging at the table, and certainly do not give into it.

Types of Food

Good-quality proprietary food is the easiest to feed. It includes all the vital nutrients in the right percentages, that includes minerals and vitamins which might be missing from a home-made eating plan of cooked or fresh meat and table scraps.

These are 4 types of commercially made food.

1. Moist or Wet Canned or Pouch Dog Food

Canned food has high water material, is offered in a wide variety of tastes and is generally the favored option of dogs.

Pros:

- Exceptionally tasty
- Long storage time if unopened
- Includes all the nutrients a dog requires

Cons:

- Heavy to carry and bulky to keep
- Strong smell
- Fattening
- Consists of lots of artificial additives
- Bad for teeth

- Costly

- Spoils rapidly

2. Semi-moist Pouch Dog Food

Typically including veggie protein such as soya, this food typically consists of less water than canned variant, and for that reason, it keeps well in a bowl without losing texture and drying.

Pros:

- Tasty

- Easier to store

- Includes all the nutrients a dog requires

Cons:

- Powerful smell

- Fattening

- Really pricey

- Bad for teeth

- Includes manufactured artificial additives

- Spoils rapidly

3. Dry Complete Dog Food

As its name recommends, this food consists of very little water and all the nutrients your dog requires. Certain types are developed to be dampened with water prior to feeding, while other types could be fed as they are, in which case your dog is going to require lots of water to drink in combination with it.

Pros:

- Low smell

- Cost-effective

- A better choice for teeth

- Consists of all the nutrients a dog requires

- Convenient

Cons:

- Goes off if kept too long

- Bulky to keep

- High cereal material can trigger issues for gluten-sensitive dogs

- Not as tasty as semi-moist/canned

4. Dry Complementary Dog Food

Created to be fed with cooked, canned or raw meat, this food generally consists of biscuits or cereal. Fed alone, it does not meet a dog's everyday dietary requirements.

Pros:

- Low smell

- Cost-effective

- The majority of them are supplemented with minerals and vitamins

- Excellent energy source

- A better choice for teeth

Cons:

- It takes a lot of time to combine with protein-giving components

- Bulky to keep

- Spoils if kept for too long

Homemade Food

A great deal of dogs take pleasure in homemade foods, however, basing an entirely balanced eating plan around these could be truly tough; a mineral and vitamin supplement is going to likely be required, too - consult your veterinarian for recommendations.

For simple feeding, especially for hectic owners, it's easier to stay with exclusive dog food and just offer a routine homemade meal for a snack, or to lure a dog that is ill and has actually lost the hunger. When it comes to the latter, products like boneless meats, cooked porridge, scrambled eggs, and fish are frequently valued and quickly absorbed. Constantly enable cooked foods to cool prior to offering.

In the following chapters, we are going to concentrate more on homemade dog food - their disadvantages and advantages, and how to make each dish delicious and excellent for your dog.

Chapter 2: Is Homemade Dog Food Any Good?

Neglect the restaurant doggie bag. Nowadays, more dogs are consuming their own patios, gulping down homemade canine food. There have actually been steady increases in the amount of individuals who are asking for aid with developing homemade eating plans for their dogs, according to most of the vets in the United States. The movement towards homemade dog food began a while back, and the huge bulk of dog owners keep on feeding their dogs commercial dog foods. The demand for homemade dog food got more potent after the spring 2007 recall of melamine-tainted pet food.

Besides item contamination scares, many dog owners think that homemade meals are a fresher choice as opposed to ready-made dog food. There are likewise pet owners who have substantial time and have a rather strong bond with their animal and feel that if they will preserve a healthy eating plan, they desire their dog to consume healthy, too.

Owners might likewise cook and prepare for their pets as an expression of love, given that a lot of pet owners see their dogs as kids.

Well balanced Diet

So you're enticed to attempt home cooking for your pooch. Precisely what should you consider?

Whether owners are getting dishes from a guidebook, the web, or by means of their veterinarian or veterinary nutritional expert, one problem tops the list. Owners want to make certain the dish will provide something that is well balanced and comprehensive to their dog. From a dietary point of view, that's the greatest barrier that somebody has when attempting to feed something homemade. There aren't any miracle foods or components for this.

Industrial dog foods are created to supply adequate nutrients. However, dog owners who prepare homemade dog food have to make sure that the eating plan consists of a carb source, a protein source, adequate minerals and vitamins, and some fat. Dogs do have a requirement for a little amount of fat.

House cooks can mix carbs and protein in a range of mixes, like rice and lamb, potatoes and beef, or pasta and chicken. Carbohydrates are an affordable source of energy and provide some crucial fats and amino acids.

In addition, a choice of veggies would be completely ideal, despite the fact that veterinarians warn about garlic and onions, since they could be harmful to dogs.

Extra foods to shield your dogs from: grapes, raisins, chocolate, macadamia nuts, and raw meat, which exposes dogs to threats, such as E. Coli and salmonella. All meat needs to be cooked effectively.

Despite the fact that owners can discover numerous dishes for homemade dog food in books and on the internet, some specialists motivate dog owners to take the dishes initially to their veterinarian and ask if their dog physician might help them identify if it's well balanced.

Furthermore, owners doing homemade eating plans need to have their dog and the eating plan examined two times a year at a minimum. Owners likewise have to bear in mind that dogs in various life phases or with health conditions could have completely various dietary requirements than a typical, healthy adult dog.

Owners can likewise look for a reliable veterinarian nutritional expert to help them to produce a well-balanced eating plan. Frequently, these professionals are offered by means of a nearby veterinarian school, or might be open to speak with your routine veterinarian by means of the web or the phone.

For dog owners who want to discover dog food dishes on the internet, websites which are run by board-certified veterinary nutritional experts are great recipe sources.

Supplementation

Do dogs consuming homemade dog food need supplements to ensure they're obtaining enough nutrients? They do.

Professionals state that dietary insufficiencies could lead to health problems. Calcium is amongst the most typical shortages in a homemade eating plan that isn't balanced well. When dogs do not obtain appropriate calcium, they're susceptible to a condition referred to as dietary secondary hyperparathyroidism, which can lead to bone injuries and soft bones.

Veterinarians have actually seen these types of outcomes on young dogs taking in out-of-balance homemade eating plans. They see problems with their bone development-- they're plainly not growing usually, hence you are going to see bent limbs, or they're actually bowed and bent. Often, it might likewise be major enough that they see real damaged bones.

Besides calcium, other minerals and vitamins are important, too, like iron, magnesium, and zinc. These nutrients have to be included, which could be really hard for homemade dog food.

Dog owners need to talk to their veterinarians with regard to supplements.

Time and Expense

It goes without saying, it's more lengthy to cook than to purchase commercial dog food at the shop. When it comes to cost, a lot is going to depend upon the dog size.

Big dogs, for instance, Rottweiler and Saint Bernard, are more pricey to feed compared to little types. In case you have a dog that's over 50 or 60 pounds.-- for example, you have 2 or more of them-- certainly, the expense is going to be higher, contrasted to the owner with 2 small Yorkies.

It's likewise crucial that owners remember to remain detailed and strictly follow the recommended dietary formula. A great deal of owners, as time passes, are going to make little changes in the eating plan due to ease of cooking or cost of components, an occasion referred to as recipe drift. You must not make these modifications without consulting a veterinarian, as they might result in poor nutrition.

Storage and Shelf-life

Packaged foods have a long shelf-life. Not so with homemade meals. The upside of homemade food is that you're selecting fresh components; the downside is that you do not have a long shelf life.

For little dogs, owners may make a huge batch, freeze it, and serve servings as needed. This will last for a long time. However, meals for big dogs are best kept in the fridge because they will probably be gone in simply a number of days.

The essential thing: Home-cooked eating plans may be extremely satisfying and healthy for owners, however, they require time dedication and additional expense from the owner, and evaluation with a veterinarian to ensure the eating plan is not triggering the dog damage.

Homemade Recipes

Which would you choose for supper - a homemade mixture in the house or a microwaveable frozen dinner? Almost everybody has actually consumed both. Chances are, whoever is preparing the homemade food may do a lot better than a frozen food brick.

Or maybe, your furry buddy is more than happy to scarf down anything which gets in his bowl. If so, you might wish to ask yourself, "Is standard dog food the ideal thing for him?" Your supper options might well be a no-brainer, however, discovering the right choice for your dog isn't normally that easy. He's depending on you to make the healthiest, and yes, the most enjoyable, choices for him.

When you make homemade food for your dog, you can be certain that your pet is consuming foods which are free from preservatives, chemicals and additives which are typically present in commercial dog foods. The huge concern is: is this sufficient to fulfill his everyday dietary requirements?

Homemade Dog Food Kinds

Yes, there are. Much like human food, homemade dog food could be categorized so as to filter the hunt for your furry buddy's ideal eating plan. However, lines might be blurred, and things can overlap. For instance, you might choose to feed a raw dog food eating plan while keeping away from all of the foods that experts have regarded as potentially harmful. Or you might select to utilize holistic health principles while utilizing natural and organic components. That is what homemade dog food is about, besides - customizing your dog's eating plan in a way that satisfies you both.

Raw Dog Food VS Biologically Appropriate Raw Food (BARF)

Your dog is a wild animal which has been domesticated. And, just like people, any species' ideal eating plan is its native one. And a dog's native eating plan is meat. Moreover, various people would confirm that raw meat is perfect.

Unlike people, dogs aren't normally susceptible to conditions such as e-coli and salmonella.

Organic Homemade Dog Food

The topic of organic foods is a pretty big one. A whole lot of individuals think that herbicides, bug killers, human waste, radiation, sewage gunge, genetic modifications, and artificial ingredients have no place on or in our vegetables and fruit. However, how about meat? Are you aware that your meat - and the meat which you give to your dog - could be natural and organic, too?

Organic meat is farmed from animals that have actually been grown lacking medicines or artificial growth hormonal agents, and have actually not been fed animal by-products. Natural and organic foods supply no more nutrition than traditional ones, however, their appeal is purely about what's NOT within them. You are going to be spending more for less, however, it's a lot less of what you do not desire and do not require. The majority of supermarkets offer organic meat these days, so discovering them will not be an issue.

Homemade Holistic Dog Food

Holistic feeding techniques and medicine are based upon the idea that feeding the body and mind aids to manage and restore vitality and health. Principles include ideals such as assortment and balance. Holistic eating plans might be offered cooked or raw - your choice.

Assortment and rotation are necessary, much like variety is essential when it comes to your own excellent eating plan routine. Holistic dog food principles claim that grains are appropriate for dogs - in line with the claim that when dogs consume wild animals, they similarly consume the stomach contents of those animals, and that includes greens and grains. Numerous holistic dog food dishes consist of one part of carbs, two parts of protein, and one part of vegetables.

Utilizing these standards, you have the ability to develop a variety of dishes.

Should You Give Supplements to Your Dog?

Though views vary substantially, it's a belief of lots of others that a healthy dog's dietary requirements could be satisfied with absolutely nothing more than exercise and food. Magnesium and Calcium levels are frequently the only 2 shortage factors to consider when it comes to a homemade dog food eating plan.

You might improve calcium with white cheese, unflavored yogurt, sardines and crushed eggshells. Vitamin D to release the calcium could be obtained from time outdoors on a warm day or cod liver oil. Magnesium is discovered in spinach and kelp, both are good options, however, just when steamed initially.

Despite the feeding principle that you choose for your dog, some things are universally agreed upon by the pros:

- Dogs require protein - vegetarian eating plans are broadly contested and do not provide total nutrition for animals which are typically meat-eating.

- Commercial dog foods that feature a lot of grains offer minimal nutrition.

- Some commercial dog foods consist of additives and a lot more ominous elements, such as by-products of sick animals, malignant tissue, shelter kills, and artificial components.

- Foods which are bad for you are probably bad for your dog as well. Sugar-laden goodies and fried foods undermine other worthy efforts and supply little if any nutrition.

Should You Be Cooking For Your Dog?

Not remarkably, you might feel stressed out about the idea of feeding your pet from your own kitchen area. Maybe you have minimal time to cook even for your own household. Consider utilizing the following time-saving tips to make your dog's longevity and health attainable:

- Rather than dicing fresh veggies, have bags of frozen ones quickly accessible.

-Utilize ready baby food rather than pureeing veggies.

- Prepare meals beforehand and freeze in individual serving sizes.

- Eat what your dog eats - create meals which everybody in the family, canine and human, can take pleasure in.

- Strike a deal with your butcher or grocer. Speak to him about what you desire, and schedule a particular week day when you have the ability to drop in and get what he's booked just for you.

- Utilize your slow cooker. Place proper components into the slow cooker prior to heading to work.

- Include the entire family.

Chapter 3: Homemade VS Store-Bought Dog Food

It is necessary to select the appropriate eating plan. This chapter explains the advantages, together with the disadvantages, of homemade and store-bought food. Is one above the other? What are the variants in between store-bought and DIY dog food? Lots of dog owners have opposing views when it comes to selecting the ideal food for their dog. These points can assist in identifying whether homemade or store-bought food is better for your dog.

Nutrition

Nutrition has to be your main aim when choosing the appropriate food for your dog. Store-bought food might seem the healthiest and the most dependable choice, nevertheless, numerous store-bought foods include chemical substances, preservatives and ingredients that aren't good for your dog. Do not presume all dog foods from the can are scrap, however, you should take a look at the labels meticulously to assist you to discover the appropriate store-bought food for your animal.

Additionally, homemade dog food does not include any chemicals and just consists of natural elements. However, if you select to create your own dog food, you need to be sure that it satisfies your dog's dietary needs. Both homemade and store-bought dog food could be healthy; however, it's your choice which you pick for feeding your dog. You need to acquire the recommendation of your veterinarian prior to choosing an eating plan for your dog.

Selection

Homemade food tends to provide a higher range of flavors and tastes than store-bought food. Store-bought dog food typically just is offered in a little selection of different tastes. If you would like your dog to enjoy a varied eating plan, you may want to consider homemade food. You are going to discover recipes for various dog treats and foods on the web. Your dog is going to get a kick out of the effort you invest in preparing tasty and new foods and treats for him to devour.

Management

If you choose to provide your dog with homemade food, you are going to have complete control of what your dog consumes daily. You can be certain that your dog does not consume any possibly unsafe ingredients. If you select to feed your dog store-bought food, you might not understand precisely what your dog takes in. If control matters to you when it pertains to your dog's eating plan, an eating plan of homemade food is going to be the ideal option.

Cost

Is there a difference in expense in between homemade and store-bought dog food? Not actually. If you choose to acquire organic and top-quality items for your homemade dog food, it is going to be expensive. If you decide to purchase the ideal, premium brand names of dog food in the shop, it is going to also be costly. If you select your components or producers wisely, you can reduce the dog food expense. Most of all, you should not haggle the wellness and health of your dog.

It's totally your decision, as the owner, whether you select to supply your dog with store-bought or homemade food. If you decide to make any modifications to your dog's present eating plan, you need to guarantee that you present brand-new foods bit by bit to stay clear of diarrhea and gastrointestinal problems.

Which Is More Affordable?

Cooking on your own is reliably less costly than purchasing ready-made food. However, how about when it comes to your pet? Whether homemade dog food costs less than store-bought is identified by a number of aspects, such as what grade of dog food you buy and what components you use for your homemade dog food.

Canned Dog Food

The expense per 12-ounce can of dog food differs extensively based upon the producer. A shop brand names and mid-range brand names charge approximately $1.25 for every can. A regular premium can of dog food costs approximately $2.50. The cost per 16 ounces for fundamental canned dog food is $1.67, and $3.33 for top-quality canned food.

Keep in mind that when you compare dog food price, you may typically feed your dog a little less with the higher-quality brand names and still provide your dog with comparable nutrients.

Dry Dog Food

Once again, the expense of dry dog food varies a lot with respect to the grade and brand name. For midrange dry food, the cost per 30-pound bag is approximately $35. Premium dry dog food averages $65 for a 30-pound bag. So, the expense per pound for dry midrange pet food is $1.17 per pound. The expense per pound for kibble is approximately $2.17.

Homemade Dog Food With Ordinary Ingredients

The possibilities are almost limitless when you're creating homemade dog food. The worth of making home-cooked dog suppers is identified by the changing rates and components you choose. Dog food dishes originate from a ratio of one-fifth grain, three-fifths meat and one-fifth vegetable.

Homemade Dog Food With Organic Ingredients

You might choose that you wish to use organic items in your house cooking to compete with the high-quality dog food brand names. The worth of organic components is reliably greater.

Myths and Misconceptions

It's been a number of years since the initial melamine-related dog food recall, and throughout that time, more dog fans than ever took an interest in homemade eating plans- raw or cooked - as protection from possible problems with commercial dog foods. Is homemade dog food truly protection from harmful canned foods? Certainly, it could be, IF it's nutritionally proportionate and accounts for your dog's age, breed, activity, weight and general make-up.

To assist dog owners who want to change to homemade eating plan for their dogs, here are 8 of the most typical misconceptions and myths about homemade dog food. Remember, however, that this goes for healthy, adult dogs.

- Utilizing balanced, fresh foods is going to, as time passes, meet my pooch's requirements if I change the diet program enough.

There are particular grounds for this understanding; fresh vegetables and fruit genuinely are more bio-available contrasted to those made with ready-made components. Moreover, when an owner preps homemade food, he/she is precisely knowledgeable about what's entering into the food. However, when analyzed, even eating plans depending upon well balanced, fresh vegetables and fruit could still appear short of the nutrient variety a dog requires.

Make-up for this by performing research on the true nutrient needs of your pooch; what this suggests is speaking with nutrition specialists, reading different books and veterinarians, and beginning to consider both dietary requirements and ingredients.

- A multi-vitamin placed into the meals is going to deal with any gaps.

The concern here is this: precisely which multi-vitamin do you utilize? Any home-prepared, un-supplemented eating plan is going to lack certain nutrients while being packed with others. However, given that there is no traditional formula for human multi-vitamins and they differ in what they include, simply tossing one in the meal isn't the remedy.

Picking an all-purpose multi made especially for dogs does not necessarily resolve the problem either. These normally consist of remarkably low levels of nutrients because it's presumed they are going to be placed into commercial food, and they are not likely to offer sufficient nutrients.

- Including yogurt to my dog's food daily meals can assist in getting her adequate calcium.

Dogs require quite high quantities of calcium, and plain yogurt absolutely WON'T qualify. Unless you want to place 40 cups of yogurt into your dog's meals daily. Calcium supplement is continuously needed if you aren't feeding raw bones.

- My individual eating plan is an outcome of a mindful research study of human nutrition books, and I simply abide by comparable guidelines with my dog.

This could be a rather normal presumption, nevertheless, it is imprecise. Present dietary standards for people aren't normally well fit for dogs.

- My dog had some soft bowels, so decreasing fiber is going to deal with that.

Fiber is a vital dietary component, and the type of fiber you utilize matters more than the amount.

In the event that your dog has soft bowels on a homemade eating plan, shift to bland meals or trim the volume of food by approximately one-third for a day or two, and search for other indications that may expose undesirable organisms or a disease. If it does not improve within a number of days, talk to your veterinarian.

- I utilize a great deal of fresh veggies in my dog's eating plan, given that they provide a variety of health advantages.

Veggies' role the dog eating plan has actually ended up being a subject of considerable discussion. One stance holds that integrating them is undesirable, considering that dogs are carnivores and do not require plant matter. Others emphasize the requirement for both fruits and veggies to enhance not simply necessary minerals and vitamins however likewise phytochemicals that might protect your animal from illness.

The important thing is that dogs' systems have a tendency to be more flexible than other animals, and veggies supply a lot when it pertains to health benefits. Once again, we're faced with the critical issues, "Just how much veggies and of what kind?" Some veggies have elements that might prevent the absorption of nutrients, yet others consist of solanine - an alkaloid that some believe worsens swelling. Deal with veggies smartly: Reduce dark leafy greens. Carrots and green beans are frequently winners, and sweet potatoes and pumpkin are successfully accepted.

- Dogs do not require carbs, and entire grains could be hazardous to them.

Dogs can process sufficient glucose from an eating plan made up of protein and fat alone.

This indicates that shortage of carbs will not lead to an identifiable deficit in the way that a lack of Vitamin C in people is going to produce. It does not, nevertheless, suggest that a carb-free eating plan is a good idea. The ideal bet is to attempt to preserve levels as they are, so if required, you might make changes.

- A raw food eating plan is typically more desirable than one that's cooked considering that dogs fed raw do not get ill.

Raw diets differ in type; some search for nutrition balance while some utilize a "prey design" method, which mimics the eating plan of wild dogs or wolves as highly as feasible. These eating plans have actually grown to be enormously popular over the past 10 years, and to be certain, there are dogs that completely flourish on them. Nevertheless, some do not. Just like a cooked eating plan, it's required to guarantee appropriate formula. Raw eating plans have drawbacks in addition to benefits, and might not be perfect for each dog.

Warning

Numerous veterinarians, while acknowledging that the poor quality of some dog foods and food recalls cause issues, still think that homemade eating plans, when fed exclusively, might result in vitamin/mineral shortages and dietary instability that might present dangers to dog health. Consequently, if you choose to feed your dog a homemade eating plan, it is important that you understand and provide what your dog requires to stay healthy; veterinarian nutritional experts can assist in producing suitable homemade eating plans. While plenty of care was provided to supply accurate guidelines and safe suggestions in this chapter, it's not feasible to determine a particular dog's reaction to any component or food. You ought to consult your veterinarian and use individual judgment when utilizing this info for your own dogs' eating plan.

Chapter 4: Recipes

Numerous ready-made dry dog foods, frequently called kibble, are packed with carcinogens, toxic substances, elements and irritants that provide your dog with insufficient base nutrition. Transforming your dog from commercially produced, extremely processed kibble to homemade dog food eater could be of substantial benefit to your dog's basic health.

Homemade dog food is probably much healthier than the ready-made dog food you may discover in the grocery store, pet shops, and veterinarian centers. Creating your own dog food, nevertheless, takes a little bit more time, however, you can create extra and keep it in the freezer.

Listed beneath are rather healthy, easy-to-make dog food dishes that you may make for your dog. The components utilized are selected to assist your dog's general health, improve his disease-fighting ability, help oral health, minimize the likelihood of cancer, and more. When purchasing the components utilized in the dishes, you may select if you wish to go organic or otherwise; however, even if you select the latter, rest assured that the recipes are thoroughly produced to be loaded with the appropriate, great nutrition every canine requires.

Veggie and Beef Balls

Some dogs favor meaty treats over sweet meals. This has a hearty meat taste and an excellent fragrance that all dogs actually take pleasure in.

You are going to require:

- 1 cup of whole-wheat flour (or white alternative).

- 2 6-ounce containers of veggie baby food and organic beef.

- 1 cup of water.

- 2 cups of dry milk.

Directions:

1. Pre-heat the oven to 350 degrees Fahrenheit.

2. Blend all of the components in a big blending bowl.

3. Drop the mix in big spoonfuls onto a flat pan.

4. Bake 15 minutes.

5. Permit the treats to totally cool.

6. Store remaining veggie balls and beef in the refrigerator for as much as 5 days.

Vegetable and Turkey Supper

This fundamental dog dish integrates turkey for protein and veggies for included minerals and vitamins.

You are going to require:

- 4 cups of water.

- 2 cups of wild rice.

- 1 cup of sliced carrots.

- 1 pound of ground turkey.

- 1 cup of sliced green beans.

- 1 tablespoon of fish oil (optional).

Directions:

1. Prepare the ground turkey in a non-stick frying pan accross medium heat up until the meat is cooked throughout.

2. Include the wild turkey, rice, and water to a big pot and bring to a boil.

3. Decrease the heat to medium-low and cook an extra 15 minutes, or up until the rice is tender and soft.

4. Include the green beans and carrots and cook for an extra 5 to 10 minutes, up until the veggies are tender.

5. Enable it to cool prior to serving.

6. Store additional suppers in the refrigerator for approximately 5 days.

Chicken Casserole

This dish uses chicken, which is an excellent source of protein, and a lot of veggies to deliver a delicious mix. Green beans assist your dog to feel satiated and veggies offer minerals and vitamins.

You are going to require:

- 4 chicken breasts
- 1/2 cup of sliced carrots
- 1/2 cup of sliced green beans
- 1/2 cup rolled oats.

- 1/2 cup of sliced broccoli

- 4 cups of low-salt chicken broth

Directions:

1. Remove excess fat from the chicken breasts and cut the breasts into little portions.

2. Prepare the chicken breasts in a non-stick frying pan over medium heat up until it is no longer pink.

3. Include the chicken, rolled oats, veggies, and chicken broth in a big pot and cook accross medium heat up until the carrots are tender - approximately 15 minutes.

4. Enable it to cool prior to offering.

5. Store remaining casserole parts in the refrigerator for as much as 5 days.

Dog Chili

Dogs need substantial quantities of protein to guarantee that they're active and healthy. Your pup should get most of his protein from entire meat resources, such as fresh chicken. Beans also have a terrific quantity of protein.

You are going to require:

- 4 chicken breasts

- 1 cup of drained black beans.

- 1 cup of drained kidney beans.

- 1/2 cup of tomato paste

- 1 cup of diced carrots.

- 4 cups of chicken broth

Directions:

1. Remove the extra fat and chop the chicken breasts into little pieces.

2. Cook the chicken breasts in a non-stick frying pan accross medium-high heat up until pink no more.

3. Include the chicken, carrots, beans, tomato paste, and chicken broth into a big pot and cook accross medium heat up until heated up throughout - approximately 10 minutes.

4. Enable the mix to cool prior to offering.

5. Store remaining chili in the refrigerator for approximately 5 days.

Peanut Butter Cookies

Dogs like peanut butter, and these cookies are a great method to slip some fish oil into your dog's eating plan. This specific oil improves your dog's coat, rendering it healthier and softer. For this dish, it's suggested to utilize natural peanut butter considering that a variety of commercial brand names of peanut butter have actually unsuited preservatives and hydrogenated oils. In case you can't locate a natural one, then simply make your own! For this, you are going to just require peanut oil and raw peanuts (and a food processor or a blender).

You are going to require:

- 2 cups of flour (white if the pooch is allergic to it, wheat if he isn't).

- 1/3 cup of smooth peanut butter.

- 1 cup of rolled oats.

- 1/2 tablespoon of fish oil.

- 1 tablespoon of honey.

- 1 1/2 cups of water.

Directions:

1. Pre-heat the oven to 350 degrees Fahrenheit.

2. Mix the oats and flour together in a big blending bowl. Pour in one cup of water and blend up until smooth. Mix the honey, peanut butter, and fish oil and mix up until all the components are well mixed.

3. Slowly include the water till the mixture has a doughy and dense consistency.

4. Slightly flour a cooking surface area. Roll the dough onto the surface area to create a 1/4 inch thick sheet.

5. Use a cookie cutter to create shapes. Place the cookies onto a flat pan and bake for 40 minutes.

6. Allow the cookies to cool totally prior to offering.

Chicken Jerky

The jerky is both hard and chewy, so it is going to keep your dog captivated for a long time. The chicken provides a helpful quantity of protein. Furthermore, this reward can likewise assist to clean up the dog's teeth.

You are going to require:

- 2 to 4 chicken breasts.

Directions:

1. Pre-heat the oven to 200 degrees Fahrenheit.

2. Remove any extra fat from the chicken. Turn the white meat on its side and utilize a paring knife to chop and divide the breast into 1/8 inch thick strips.

3. Set the strips on a flat pan. Bake for 2 hours.

4. Evaluate the chicken prior to taking it out from the oven. It needs to be tough and dry. Enable the chicken to cool totally prior to offering.

5. Stock the jerky snack in an airtight container/jar within the refrigerator. You may offer this to your dog up to 2 weeks.

Frozen Yogurt Pops

This cool homemade delight is constructed out of human-grade components and includes carrots and fruit juice, which offer your four-legged buddy an additional vitamin increase. Yogurt has protein and calcium, and assists your dog in breaking the food down.

You are going to require:

- 6 oz. container of NON-FAT, plain frozen yogurt

- 1/2 cup of minced carrots

- 1 cup of "no-sugar-added" fruit juice

Directions:

1. Include the fruit juice, yogurt, and carrots into a bowl. Blend up until the components are smooth and well-blended.

2. Place the mix into the ice trays.

3. Freeze up until the mixes are strong.

Vegetable and Fruit Strips

These strips function as a more inexpensive replacement for the chewy organic delight offered in pet shops. Furthermore, they disintegrate easily, so you may offer tinier pieces as training treat. Veggies and fruits are plentiful with vitamin C, which may enhance your dog's bodily defense mechanisms.

You are going to require:

- 1 medium banana
- 1 little sweet potato
- 1/2 cup unsweetened natural applesauce
- 1 cup minced carrots
- 1 cup of rolled oats.
- 2 cups of entire wheat flour (white if your pooch is allergic).
- 1/3 cup of water.

Directions:

1. Prepare the sweet potato in the microwave 10 minutes, or up until the inner portions are soft. Place aside and enable it to cool.

2. Pre-heat the oven to 350 degrees Fahrenheit.

3. Mash the sweet potato and banana in a big blending bowl with a hand masher up until smooth. Include the flour, carrots and oats.

Slowly include the water and applesauce while blending.

4. The components are going to form a soft dough. Roll the dough on to a gently floured surface area up until it is 1/8 inch thick.

5. Slice the dough into strips.

6. Cook on a flat pan for half an hour.

7. Stock remaining strips in the refrigerator for approximately 2 weeks.

While lots of dogs can handle a variety of various treats provided in tiny amounts, some might get indigestion if you change foods prematurely or exceedingly. Before beginning making your own dog food at home, talk with your veterinarian and ask if he/she has any particular component suggestions, as some dog types might be more prone to food allergic reactions than others. After getting your veterinarian's approval, change your dog's food gradually, slowing mixing in a homemade meal with your routine food for several days.

Chapter 5: Foods to Give/Avoid

When you see your dog with a small look while standing close to the table, you might be inclined to slip your furry buddy a piece of your food. Sharing food with your dog might seem relatively benign, however, beyond promoting bad pleading routines and even gaining weight, you might basically be putting your dog's life and health at risk.

There are a range of components and foods consumed by people daily, like milk, chocolate and garlic that can cause serious poisonous responses in dogs. In this chapter, we will take specific notice of the ones which could be most harmful to your four-legged buddy.

People Foods That are Safe for Dogs

There are people food products which are fine to feed to your dog; nevertheless, these products need to be kept as little as feasible. These products are:

Lean Meat

Lean meat includes meat without bones that has actually had all the additional fat removed. If feeding turkey and chicken, the skin needs to likewise be taken out as it could be a fat source. Lean meat consists of white meat from turkey or chicken and is a yummy delight for your dog along with being an exceptional protein source.

Raw (and cooked) Eggs

The most obvious issue here is salmonella, however, raw eating plan enthusiasts promote the raw egg effectiveness in your dog's eating plan. While the white supplies the Avidin enzyme, which stops the vitamin B (Biotin) absorption, the yolk consists of more than adequate Biotin to cancel the enzyme. So, when fed whole and raw, or whole and cooked, eggs are filled with protein and a host of natural vitamins.

Fruits

Dogs can harmlessly relish in bananas, strawberries, apples, watermelon and blueberries. The seeds need to be removed from these fruits, or when it comes to watermelon, it needs to be a seedless one as many fruit seeds have arsenic that is harmful. Fresh fruits are an exceptional snack to assist in training your dog and can also offer your dog an excellent way to cool off throughout the summertime.

Veggies

Some veggies such as green beans, carrots, zucchini or cucumber pieces are all outstanding snacks for your dog. It's wise to use baby carrots instead of commercial dog treats if you wish to thin your dog down a tad. Veggies make a fantastic low-calorie snack, and excellent training tools too. However, avoid marinaded and canned veggies considering that they have a lot of salt.

Baked potatoes

A plain baked potato is great to feed your dog, however, in all sincerity, it's not a thing that should be done frequently and must never ever consist of any garnishes. A couple of pieces of prepared baked potato could be an excellent snack for a pup that is patient enough.

Pasta and White Rice

Pasta and white rice are typically seen as a possible meal for a dog with indigestion. Usually, white rice and white chicken are utilized to assist firm up stools together with support a dog which is having trouble obtaining any nutrition from food due to disease.

While there are certainly some human foods that are harmless to offer your dog, there are many which are harmful and possibly toxic when taken in by your dog. Usually speaking, it's better being safe than sorry, so stay away from feeding your dog any human food unless, naturally, recommended by your veterinarian.

Dogs that aren't provided table scraps or human food are typically much better behaved than dogs who do obtain individuals food somehow, they do not plead considering that they understand they will not obtain any scraps and they likewise tend to drool less and trouble visitors to your house less considering that they comprehend that human food is for humans and not them.

Risky Human Food

Alcohol

Alcohol can lead to not simply intoxication, bad breathing, loss of coordination, and irregular acidity level, however, perhaps even coma and/or death.

Apple Seeds

Apple seeds are hazardous to a dog as they consist of a natural chemical which discharges cyanide when taken in. So, ensure to seed and core apples prior to offering to your pooch.

Avocado

Avocados have Persin, which may trigger queasiness, diarrhea, and heart blockage.

Baby food

Baby food alone isn't bad, simply make certain it does not consist of any sort of onion powder. Baby food likewise does not have all the nutrients a dog depends upon for a clean, healthy eating plan.

Bones

The danger with bones isn't the dietary material, nor is it constantly the risk of choking. Rather, you need to beware when it comes to bones from meat sources such as fish and chicken because they might harm your dog's gastrointestinal system once the bones splinter within the body.

Sweet and Gum

Besides sweet consisting of sugar; it typically has Xylitol, which may lead to kidney failure, over-release of insulin, and even worse, death.

Cat food

Not that the dog would desire this at any rate, however, cat food has fats and proteins that are aimed at the eating plan of a cat, NOT a dog. The fat and protein levels in cat food are far too strong for your pooch, therefore, making it unhealthy for dogs.

Chocolate

You have actually most likely heard this in the past, however, chocolate is a CERTAIN NO-NO for dogs. And it's not just about caffeine, which is sufficient to trigger damage to your dog alone, however, theophylline and theobromine, which is typically harmful, lead to throwing up, panting, and diarrhea, and hinder your dog's nerve system and heart.

Citrus Extracts

Results in throwing up.

Coffee

The guidelines and info here are practically identical as the guidelines and info versus chocolate. This is essentially toxic for your dog if taken in.

Corn on the Cob

This is a sure-fire technique of blocking your dog's intestinal tract. The corn is absorbed, however, the cob becomes stuck in the tiny intestine, and if it's not removed surgically, it may be deadly to your dog. In addition, extreme corn kernels may distress the gastrointestinal system too.

Fat Trimmings

Causes pancreatitis.

Fish

The primary fish you have to be careful with are trout and salmon. Raw salmon may be lethal to dogs if the fish is polluted with a particular parasite, Nanophyetus salmincola. The parasite by itself isn't damaging to dogs, however, it is typically contaminated with germs referred to as Neorickettsia helminthoeca, which often is deadly for dogs if not handled properly. Nevertheless, cooked salmon is fine as it eliminates the parasite.

Grapes and Raisins

This is one which a variety of dog owners do not know. Grapes have a toxic substance which causes kidney failure and liver damage.

Human Vitamins

Certain people vitamins are appropriate to utilize, however, the crucial thing is examining the components (each of them - non-active and active) and the vitamins your veterinarian assigns to your dog. Ensure there's no iron, as this can damage the gastrointestinal system lining, and end up being poisonous for the kidneys and liver.

Liver

Avoid feeding excessive liver to your pooch. Liver includes a considerable quantity of Vitamin A, which may detrimentally impact your puppy's bones and muscles.

Macadamia Nuts

These have a contaminant that can decrease locomotory activities, resulting in panting, lethargy, inflamed limbs, and tremors, together with feasible injury to your dog's gastrointestinal, muscular and nervous systems.

Milk and Dairy

While little dosages aren't probable to end your dog's life, you may get some foul-smelling farts and some horrible instances of diarrhea. Dogs are lactose-intolerant, and do not have adequate amount of lactase enzyme to absorb dairy foods efficiently. If you have to provide dairy, think about lactose-free items.

Mushrooms

Much like the incorrect mushroom could be lethal to people, the identical pertains to dogs.

Onions, Garlic, and Chives

No matter what form they remain in (raw, dry, powder, cooked, within other foods), garlic and onions (especially onions) are amongst the outright worst foods you might provide your puppy. These are toxic to dogs. They consist of sulfoxides (thiosulphate) and disulfides, both can ruin red blood cells and trigger anemia.

Persimmons, Peaches, and Plums

If you live in a location in which is home to peach, persimmon, or plum trees, beware. Persimmon seeds and peach and plum pits result in enteritis and digestive blockage. You have to guarantee there aren't any wild persimmon or other fruit trees which leave seeds growing in your lawn.

Rhubarb and Tomato leaves

These consist of oxalates which may detrimentally affect the nervous, gastrointestinal, and urinary systems.

Raw fish

Yet another vitamin B (Thiamine) deficit may arise from the routine raw fish consumption. Appetite loss is going to be common, in addition to seizures, and death, in extraordinary circumstances.

Salt

Just like salt isn't the healthiest product for individuals, it's much less healthy for dogs. An extreme quantity of it may lead to dehydration, an imbalance in electrolyte levels, and potentially diarrhea.

Sugar

This applies to any food which contains sugar. Ensure you verify the label with ingredients for human foods - corn syrup may be discovered in practically all the things nowadays. An extreme quantity of sugar for your dog may lead to weight problems, oral problems, and often diabetes.

Tobacco

A main poisonous hazard for dogs. The effects nicotine has on dogs is significantly worse than on people. Nicotine harms your puppy's nerve and gastrointestinal systems, makes them faint, increases their heart rate, and ultimately results in death.

Xylitol

A sugar alcohol present in sweets, gum, baked products, and other sugar-substituted items, Xylitol, while inducing no evident injury to people, is extremely harmful to dogs. Even a percentage causes convulsions, low blood sugar, liver failure, and even death.

Yeast (by itself or in dough)

Similar to yeast going up in bread, it is going to similarly rise and broaden within your puppy's stomach. Ensure they do not get any. While moderate cases are going to lead to lots of farting, gas, and distress - an extreme quantity of it might burst their stomach and intestinal tracts.

Old Food

You never ever want musty and old food, so what in the world makes you believe your dog is going to? The germs in ruined food is comprised of all kind of contaminants which are generally harmful to your dog's health. Provide just the best dog-approved food.

Leftovers

If you feed them leftovers often, they are not going to have a suitable eating plan. If you do provide table scraps, make sure to trim the fat and clear away any bones.

Take a look at the Ingredients

The last point here is making certain to understand what remains in the food you are offering your dog. The food products abovementioned must NOT be present. You'd be surprised at the amount of foods which contain caffeine and sugar, that you just would not anticipate without initially inspecting the list of ingredients.

Human Snacks

Chips may have onion and garlic powder, cookies might have chocolate, raisins, or macadamia nuts. There is an explanation why there are snacks and foods made especially for dogs.

When In Doubt, Talk to a Veterinarian

If your pooch is acting strangely, or experiencing even small indications like the absence of coordination, weakness, diarrhea, queasiness, and so on and you believe he might have consumed something he should not have, go to the veterinarian immediately. If you wait for too long, your dog might not make it.

I hope that you enjoyed reading through this book and that you have found it useful. If you want to share your thoughts on this book, you can do so by leaving a review on the Amazon page. Have a great rest of the day.

Printed in Great Britain
by Amazon